AF444299

Credits

Special thanks to Kimberly O'Bryant for her input and guidance.

Heather Gann and her design studio, *Heather Gann Designs.*

Clatsop County Historical Society

The Daily Astorian

The Astoria Public Library

Renato Rodriguez of the *Oregon Historical Society*

Gina Bardi of the *San Francisco Maritime National Historical Park Research Center*

Nehalem Historical Society

Copyright © 2024 SamAndi Publishing, LLC

captaindan@samandi.net

All rights reserved. This book or any portion thereof may not be reproduced or used in any manner whatsoever without the express written permission of the publisher except for the use of brief quotations in a book review.

Printed by Ingram Spark.

Francis H. Leggett

For all of those interested in truth and historical twists,

I present for readership evidence to understand Oregon's greatest maritime disaster from a new lens.

I have an extensive background in the maritime industry as a commercial fisherman and survived a time that saw much loss, mostly in the Bering Sea during the 1980's and 90's.

As I started researching the sinking of the *Francis H. Leggett* I noticed an old familiar pattern. In my own experience as soon as a loss of a vessel is recorded the insurance companies immediately start trying to mitigate the amount of the payouts.

Admiralty Law has been around for centuries and was written and enacted into law mostly by the shipping industry for the benefit of the vessel owners. *Acts of God,* such as storms, or rogue waves and/or shifting the blame to an employee is a common tactic used to reduce the owners' liability.

Early and historic newspaper reports of this true story are almost comical in the lengths the owners went to shift the blame away from poor maintenance. I am hoping my version, which is different from anything else I have read on the sinking of the *Francis H. Leggett,* will finally set the record straight.

I hope you enjoy the viewpoint from the Skipper's seat!

Captain Daniel C. Marvin

What are the chances?

My inspiration for this book

What are the chances,
when you are asking for a sign?

What are the chances,
It would come so soon and be so apparent?

What are the chances,
a brilliant flash of gold light,
the most beautiful thing you have ever seen!

What are the Chances,
It would show you the way to a place,
where you will find other people like you,
and you no longer feel so alone,

What are the chances?
A million to one!

Dan Marvin

Cape Meares Lighthouse,

Dan Marvin

Unraveling the Mystery

I came across this story totally by accident as I was searching through old microfiche tapes at the local Astoria library for information on the early days of the **Columbia River Lightship**. The more I read, the more fascinated I became with the sinking of the **Francis H. Leggett**. I have lived on the north Oregon coast for over forty-five years, and I am surprised how little we know about Oregon's worst maritime disaster. I had never heard anything about the disaster even though I have operated boats close to the site of the wreck.

I am going to spend a little time going through what I learned about this tragedy. Boats just do not sink, there is always a chain of events leading up to such an incident. The ship was not that old, so I went back to the beginning looking for the *signal flags,* and I will let everyone come to their own conclusions after presenting my take. The following was the first article I came across, so of course, after, I had to continue reading. I also noticed every article I read in various newspapers across the country was based on a few accounts presented by local Astoria reporters of that time. I felt incredibly lucky to come across the original statements from survivors and rescuers hidden away on these old microfiche tapes that tell a different story than what many newspaper articles and current books show.

Morning Astorian

REPORT SAYS LEGGETT SUNK

MANY PASSENGERS REPORTED ABOARD

Wireless Reaching Here Says

Only That Vessel Is in Trouble

60 Miles south

PORTLAND, Ore Sept 18---1914

A wireless sent by an unknown vessel off the Columbia River to Astoria and transmitted here, said the steam schooner Francis H. Leggett had sunk 60 miles south of the Columbia. The vessel carries passengers and was bound from Seattle to San Francisco via Aberdeen. The wireless reported her at 8 o'clock last night off the Columbia. The weather bureau reports a 40-mile gale blowing from the south.

At 7 o'clock last evening this office was apprised, through the courtesy of Colonel Ludlow, commanding officer at Fort Stevens, of the fact that the wireless at that point, had picked up a message from the sea, announcing the well-known steamer Francis H. Leggett formally of the Hammond fleet was in grave distress 50 miles down the coast: but that the S. O. steamship El Segundo then 25 miles away, had received the word of her trouble and was hastening to the Leggett's relief.

No further word has been attainable here though every effort has been made.

The Leggett is known to have passed the mouth of the Columbia River at 8 o'clock on Thursday night bound evidently for San Francisco and from Puget Sound. It is admitted that she had made astonishingly slow progress in the 22 hours intervening, it is admitted, as she is a very powerful and reasonably fast vessel. Engine trouble is held to be accountable.

The ship is of 1606 gross tons and 975 net tons; and was built at Newport News Shipyard in 1904 and is owned by the Hicks-Hauptman Transportation company, of San Francisco, and is 241.5 feet long: 42 feet beam and at 14.8 feet draft. She is under the command of Captain Charles Moro and carries a crew of 26 men and officers.

It is understood the wireless call was relayed to Fort Stevens by some cruiser off the coast, but it is not known which one.

At First Glance

It was the beginning of a new class of lumber ships that were phasing out the old sailing lumber shooners. A sturdy ship was built at the well-known and regarded Newport News Shipyard on Chesapeake Bay in 1903 for a wealthy east coast wholesale grocer named Francis H. Leggett. He'd recently invested in Andrew Hammonds' new business, The Hammond Lumber Company seeing a good business opportunity.

Leggett and Hammond met in Astoria where Leggett had been a major buyer of Columbia River canned salmon for decades. In the early 1890's Andrew Hammond had come west from Montana after hearing of a failed railroad project in which he struck an agreement with community leaders to finish a railroad line from Goble to Astoria, a distance of approximately fifty miles in return for large swaths of prime timber and other considerations. The rail line was completed in 1898 and the year following, 1899, partnered with Francis H. Leggett and cannery owner Samuel Elmore forming Columbia River Packers Association. This brought almost half of the lower river canneries under one roof and provided Leggett with a steady stream of product. Hammonds' railroad passed each cannery placing him in the position of a financial monopoly on shipping.

 In 1900 Hammond expanded his business by buying a lumber mill in Humboldt County, California, forming The Hammond Lumber Company in 1901. Francis Leggett was a large investor in this venture.

The *Francis H. Leggett* Launched

Special to The New York Times.

"Newport News, Va., Jan 31. --- The lumber steamship Francis H. Leggett was launched at the shipyard to-day at 11 o'clock. The vessel is being built for the Hammond Lumber Company of San Francisco, Cal., and it will ply in the redwood lumber trade along the California coast. Mrs. Archer M. Huntingdon. Daughter of the President of the company was the sponsor and broke a bottle of wine upon the prow of the vessel. On the ways vacated by the Leggett the keel for the battleship Louisiana, sister ship of the Connecticut, will be laid in a few days."

Francis H. Leggett, *Public Domain*

The Francis H. Leggett's hull is an interesting design with large cutouts in the bulwarks on either side of the hatch covers. I immediately thought this looked like a flaw, but the ship was designed to carry a deck load. The following pictures of the ship show she is fully loaded and the amount of *freeboard* which is the distance between the water surface and the deck of the ship. The stacks of secured lumber fill in these cuts-outs in the bulwarks.

There would be a bulkhead ahead of the large smokestack separating the engine room from the aft cargo hold. Along with another bulkhead, or multiple, under the superstructure, separating the aft cargo hold from the forward, and finally, another one about halfway between the forward cut-out and the bow. Ahead of that would be the anchor-chain locker, and above that, the forepeak, used for storage of deck equipment and miscellaneous items. I know if the shipping industry is new to you this takes a little imagination or perhaps you can draw a diagram!

After being outfitted and loaded for her two-month voyage around Cape Horn and just days out of Newport News, the **Francis H. Leggett** encountered her first gale. It is common for new vessels to have problems on their maiden voyage. The term "Shipped" is referring to large volumes of seawater that broke over the ship during the gale.

New Lumber Ship Francis H. Leggett in a Gale off Hatteras

By Telegraph to the *Morning Star*

Newport News, Va, April 29.

The new lumber ship Francis H. Leggett, from Newport News to San Francisco, returned to port this morning, having been barely crippled in a gale off Hatteras. On her voyage out to her home port she ran into a nasty norther. Her steering gear broke and the vessel, which has very little free board, shipped a quantity of water. With difficulty she was brought about and proceeded to the ship yard here for repairs. The Leggett had on board thirteen hundred tons of steel rails and two locomotives for the Hammond Lumber Company.

Repairs were made and she resumed her long voyage to the southern tip of South America, Cape Horn and then turned north up the pacific coastline to her new homeport of San Francisco, California. This was prior to the construction of the Panama Canal, which started May 4th, 1904, and finished August 15th, 1914.

Photo Credit, San Francisco Maritime National Historical Park

I like the nice high bow of **Francis H. Leggett**. It looks like she has adequate shear to force the waves to the side when bucking into it, like how a snowplow works, this design would protect the forward deck area from all but the biggest waves. The wheelhouse is high and has great visibility, the walkways around the outside give an almost perfect view of the whole deck. She has accommodations for passengers, and I am assuming they would be berthed in the superstructure under the wheelhouse, with the crew occupying the area above the noisy engine area in the stern.

The captain and mate would have staterooms behind the wheelhouse for easy access. I see two large lifeboats aft and two smaller launch type boats on either side of the wheelhouse and by 1914 she was equipped with the *Marconi Wireless Morse Code System.* She was powered by an oil fed reciprocating steam engine that was rated at 1000hp and that was coupled to a single propeller!

San Francisco and all the big cities in southern California were growing rapidly and they needed lumber for building and Andrew Hammond had big plans to ship massive amounts of logs from the Pacific Northwest and had already built a lumber mill in southern California.

When she joined the San Francisco fleet she was one of the first new lumber ships outfitted with a special purpose towing winch and at first, I thought this might be a *flag,* since towing puts a lot of stress on the propulsion machinery. But the ship was built with this purpose in mind. Leggett and Hammond knew exactly what they were doing, even the cut-outs in the bulwarks seem to match the dock heights of the little mills along the Pacific coast. So, for now I will leave it undecided.

By the end of the year, the Monday, December 21st, 1903, edition of the *Oregonian* reported that:

"It is reported from San Francisco that the Hammond Lumber Company will build two new steamers to run in the coasting trade in connection with the Francis H. Leggett, which was built In the East for the company about a year ago. According to the San Francisco papers one of the steamers will be built on this Coast, and the other In the East. The Francis Leggett has proved to be very economical and [a] handy vessel to operate and the new additions to the Hammond fleet will be of a similar type. While built primarily for the lumber trade, the Leggett has proved a very good general cargo boat. She has made but one trip to Portland and in addition to miscellaneous cargo carried -SO0, -W feet of lumber. It is reported that she will came to Portland within a few days to load grain for San Francisco."

N
NW
NE
W
E
SW
SE
S

Francis H. Leggett tied up in Newport and appears to be loading cut lumber.

The small horizontal wire between the two front masts is most likely the antennae for the *Marconi Wireless System* and indicates the wireless room was located in the middle superstructure.

Photos credits, Oregon Historical Society

The Benson Cigar Rafts

These were massive rolls, not of tobacco, but of giant logs, chained and hitched up behind ships, to tow millions of board feet down the coast. Dubbed the "Benson Raft," after Simon Benson, a wealthy, Portland timber man. The huge seaworthy rafts were used to transport massive loads of timber to the swiftly growing town of San Diego.

This operation was much cheaper than it would have been to transport by ship or by rail, and there was a fortune to be made, so Benson sat down to design a raft appropriate for large hauls, that could withstand the beating of the bar and the ocean voyage. Rafting logs was not a new idea and Robertson and Bain were making log rafts as early as 1885, but Benson figured out an ingenious and nearly foolproof design with only four rafts, out of hundreds of voyages being lost.

Benson hired John A. Festabend to man the project of putting the rafts together, at Wallace Slough at the mouth of the Claskanie River, and just off Beaver Slough at Columbia River, mile 50. The rafts were floated down 1,100 miles to San Diego in just about 15 days' time!

The Oregon Historical Society explains how the rafts were built similarly to a log ark, by making a frame of tree length logs, and then filling in the hull. A floating derrick was then used to fill the ship-like log structure and all sizes of timber could be fit inside, along with other building materials like shingles and fence posts. Chains were then used to secure the logs with one running lengthwise through the center, and several around the craft every 15 feet or so, strategically placed, as per Benson's specific design.

Once filled, the massive rafts were pushed out, and once in the water, the buoyancy of the logs would cause them to flatten out, which further tightened the chain lashings. This gave them the stability they needed in order to be towed across the bar and out in the open ocean.

To put into perspective just how big these rafts were it took four to seven weeks just to fill one after the initial basket hull was built! Joshua Binus, writing for the Oregon Historical Society, offers dimensions of just how large these rafts were, carrying 4 to 6 million feet of timber and measuring about, "800 to 1000 feet long, 55 feet wide, and 35 feet thick from top to bottom– usually drafting 26 to 28 feet deep. Holding them together was anywhere from 175 to 250 tons of chain." Huge! Now, we'll take a look at a boat hauling these massive loads. In 1907, the ***Francis H. Leggett*** happened to be towing the largest load to date.

Francis H Leggett *in San Francisco Bay towing a Benson Cigar Raft that most likely originated from the Columbia River.*

Circa 1904-1910

Photo Credits, San Francisco Maritime National Historical Park

Operational Timeline to Disaster

By the **12th of Sept 1904,** in its first full year of operation, *Francis H. Leggett* had delivered its fourth Benson Cigar Raft to San Francisco, a great start to a new business venture and she stayed busy over the next five years.

24th July 1906, *Francis H. Leggett* delivered a much-needed raft holding almost nine million board feet of mostly pilings to Mission Bay. Work in the area had come to a halt for the lack of materials.

9th July 1907, a San Francisco paper reported the *Francis H. Leggett* carrying 1,450,000 BF (Board Feet) including a deck load and towing a Benson Cigar raft holding 10,000,000 BF that was 750 feet long by 55 feet wide and 23 feet deep, had encountered a gale out of the SE, and hove to for twenty-four hours! During this time, the ship and raft drifted north forty miles. For those in the know, *hove to*, is a nautical term for drifting, or removing all sources of propulsion, this could be sail or power. The drift rate of 1.67 knots, and the fact she kept her deck load in a gale, is important.

13th Sept 1907, *Francis H. Leggett* delivered the largest log raft to date, one of eight hundred feet long, 60 feet wide, 24 feet deep and contained an estimated 11,000,000 board feet (BF) of logs while also carrying a full load of 1.6 million BF of cut lumber in her holds, and on deck! Insane!

Now, we need to question if Hammond, Leggett, and the marine architects who designed the ship, realized just how big these rafts would become in such a short time? I am not familiar with steam engines, but a 1000 horsepower engine seems very small for towing such a large raft and the only way to increase power would be to re-wheel the ship, to add pitch to the propeller. Normally, doing this means you give up speed, and the added power and thrust can put stress on the steering gear.

You can see the Hammond Lumber Company's logo, white with a red stripe on the stack in many pictures.

George W. Fenwick

George W. Fenwick, a slightly larger, Newport News Shipyard build. A sister-ship to *Francis H. Leggett* and owned by *Hammond Lumber*, crossing the Columbia River Bar with a Benson Cigar raft in tow. She was sold to a Chinese Company in 1939, and just three years later was lost after being torpedoed by a Japanese submarine during the Second World War.

Photo credit Oregon Historical Society.

Warning Flags

Small Craft, Gale, Storm, Hurricane

For those in the know, these are Coast Guard Warning Flags used to warn mariners of hazardous conditions on the ocean: Small Craft, Gale, Storm, and Hurricane. Below I have laid out the flags as they presented themselves to me, while researching the sinking.

29th Aug 1909, Francis Leggett, the grocer, collapsed and died in NYC. There were only two heirs to his estate, his fifteen-year-old daughter and her mother, who likely didn't want anything to do with a ship. (*Small Craft—red flag because ownership switches and heirs have expectations, etcetera*).

29th July 1911, remnants of a large log raft, that were lost by the ***Francis H. Leggett*** a few weeks earlier, were towed into San Francisco Bay, by the steamer ***Nehalem*** which was consigned to the *Hammond Lumber Company*.
(*Small Craft—red flag because it shows the Leggett is now replaceable*).

15th November 1911, *Hammond Lumber* sells the ***Francis H. Leggett*** *to Hicks-Hauptman Lumber Co.* of San Francisco. Two new ocean-going tugs named ***Dauntless*** and ***Hercules*** join the *Hammond Lumber* fleet, this is the end of the lucrative Benson Cigar Rafts towing contracts (*Gale flag warning!*).

25th January 1912, *The Victoria Daily Times* reports in an article titled, *"Helplessly Adrift and in Bad Place off Cape Flattery: Francis Leggett Nearly Driven Ashore Off Cape Flattery Yesterday Afternoon."* ***Francis H. Leggett*** had broken down twelve miles SW of Cape Flattery and was adrift for more than four hours with faulty steering gear. The paper also reported the steamer ***Umatilla*** stood by her until she was able to make repairs and continue under her own power. (*Gale flag warning*).

26th January 1912, the following day ***Francis H. Leggett*** docks in Astoria, and denies the report of faulty steering gear off Cape Flattery. The captain reports a broken pipe had allowed seawater to enter a fuel tank, and they needed to allow the water to separate from the fuel. The master of the ship, Captain Hall, denies even seeing the ***Umatilla*** the day before. (*Gale flag warning, shows the ship is having mechanical issues and the owners are trying to cover this up*).

Just prior to the ***Francis H. Leggett*** loss was the sinking of the ***Titanic*** which set the legal precedence for this era of the maritime industry.

14th April 1912, Her Majesty's Ship *HMS Titanic* was on her maiden voyage and was steaming full speed on a flat calm night when she strikes an iceberg in the north Atlantic. She sinks by the bow until the stern lifts out of the water and then breaks away, sinking in two sections with massive loss of life. The eyewitness accounts of the sinking were confirmed by deep sea submersibles, seventy-three years later.

The first newspaper reports of the *Titanic* sinking were chaotic with various accounts of what happened, almost all of what's reported is proven to be false later. Within a week, the winter transit lanes are moved one hundred and fifty miles south, to ice-free open water, and hearings begin to find fault. Marconi himself testified he allowed his wireless operators to sell the contents of telegrams that had been sent by the *Titanic's* owners, to other ships in the fleet and to the newspapers, following the sinking. The practice was immediately stopped upon his testimony and all telegrams, even though sent over an open-air wave, were now considered private property of the ship owner.

The insurance companies settle with the ships' owner *White Star* within a month. The shipping industry and the maritime insurance companies are mutually dependent on each other--they don't exist without one another, and to keep premiums low the insurance company will take extraordinary steps to minimize the payouts to crew and passengers. The owners of the ships won't argue, since higher payouts will result in higher premiums for the vessel owners. The stakes were huge in the case of the *Titanic* with liability claims that amounted to over 19 million dollars, with *White Star* arguing the ship was state of the art and the iceberg was an *"Act of God,"* and they had no control over the sinking. After almost eighteen months of litigation going as high as the United States Supreme court, *Lloyd's of London*, the insurance carrier, was successful, and reduced the payout by ninety-five percent!

The Groundwork for SOLAS (Safety of Life at Sea) was also laid, an international regulatory committee that sets minimum standards for ships design, construction, operation, and safety.

Over and over, I have seen this, there must be a loss to ensure change.

Continuation of "*Flags*"

12th July 1913, The ***Francis H. Leggett,*** under the command of a Captain Belleson, rams and sinks the ***J.H. Lunsmann*** in San Francisco Bay, with faulty steering gear blamed on the ***Francis H. Leggett*** (*Storm red flag warning--seeing some serious maintenance problems now*).

From the Pacific Marine Review in 1913:

*"**July 12th for Portland.** Was in a collision at 1 a.m. on the 13th with the **Schr. J.H. Lunsmann** at anchor off Black Point and was considerably damaged. She returned to port for repairs, which is estimated will cost about $8,000. The Local Inspectors are investigating as to the cause of the collision and ascertain that the steam leading to the steam steering gear had been turned off for some reason by the second engineer and the steamer failed to answer her helm in time to avoid the collision..."*

*"**J.H. Lunsmann Schr.** From Newcastle, April 12th with a cargo of coal. While lying at anchor off Black Point, San Francisco, was run into on the morning of July 12th by the Str. **"Francis H. Leggett,"** outward bound, and was sunk. Efforts are now being made by the Whitelaw Wrecking Co. to raise her.*

The sunken schooner J. H. Lunsmann as she appeared yesterday in the stream off Fort Mason, after having been rammed by the steamer Francis H. Leggett.

Sept 24th, 1913, *The Bloomington Record,* a newspaper in Wisconsin reported that Earl S. Hicks, thirty-five years old, a former lumber man of Wisconsin, and now of San Francisco, shot himself while alone at home. He had been suffering from ill health and business problems. He was the General Manager and part owner of *Hicks-Hauptman Lumber Company* of San Francisco (*Hurricane*).

Nov 16, 1913, the **Francis H. Leggett** is leased to the *Charles R. McCormick Lumber Co* of San Francisco on a one-year contract. *McCormick* brings in one of their top captains, a young well-regarded Captain Charles Maro. He had worked his way up through the *McCormick* fleet starting with the steamer **Yellowstone** followed by **Klamath, Multnomah, Yosemite,** and finally the **Francis H. Leggett.**

Without knowing the terms of the lease agreement, we do not know if *Hicks-Hauptman* or *Charles H. McCormick* companies were responsible for making major repairs. Usually when companies send a top captain, they are interested in buying the vessel and just wanted his opinion, but it's obvious with Hicks' death, *Hicks-Hauptman* is in deep financial trouble (*Hurricane*).

McCormick Lumber Co also leased four other ships from *Hicks-Hauptman.* They are the **Temple E. Dorr, Nehalem, J. B. Stetson,** *and* the Schooner **Forest Home.**

Morning Astorian

The steamer Francis H. Leggett left out from here on Sunday cargoed with lumber for San Francisco delivery.

The fourth of the Benson log rafts for the 1914 season came down from Wallace Slough on Saturday night and is still at the Flavel dolphins, but is to sail today on the towline of the San Francisco tug Dauntless, for San Diego.

Clatsop County Historical Society

Even though it says the **Francis H. Leggett** left for San Francisco, she turned north to *Grays Harbor* to finish off her deck load of railroad ties, and this was her last visit to the Columbia River.

I find it ironic that just below this notice was the **Dauntless** who took away the Leggett's lucrative towing contracts, which seemed to trigger the cascade of events that led to her loss.

Survivor accounts state **Francis H. Leggett** left *Grays Harbor* on Wednesday, court filings from a later date, months after the sinking, confirm that she left on Thursday Sept 17th, 1914.

Information which most likely came from the mill at Hoquiam, and I find no reason to question it as the timeline wouldn't work otherwise. She passed the *Columbia River* at 8 pm that evening, which came from a written log at the wireless station with no mention of poor weather, or mechanical troubles.

From the **Columbia River Lightship** to where the trouble started was about sixty-five miles south, and this is where there is a hole in the timeline.

What I have read are multiple variations of newspaper articles of Captain Maro leaving *Grays Harbor* with an overloaded ship, knowing a fierce storm was approaching and yet he continued to slam into building seas coming down the coast. By the next morning, the seas were mountainous, and the deck load shifted, causing the ship to list. Captain Maro then ordered the deck load jettisoned while he was still charging into enormous seas, and shortly after, a massive wave broke over the ship sweeping away the hatch covers and sealing her fate.

As a captain myself, with lots of heavy weather experience these articles made no sense and I asked myself, *"Why doesn't he just turn the ship around and restack the load?"*

To insinuate Captain Maro sent his crew out on deck to jettison a shifting deck load of railroad ties, while still pushing ahead in enormous seas to meet a delivery schedule that doesn't seem to exist, makes no sense whatsoever.

My biggest problem was trying to peel back all the layers of drama and mistruths that were added by the various newspapers. Someone in Astoria got a fairly accurate statement from survivor Alex Farrell, but this story was chopped into pieces, before being handed over to the media, and it was then modified to fit the readership.

E. M. Cherry, Lloyd's agent, as local representative of Hicks-Hamptman Transportation company, of San Francisco, yesterday received telegraphic instructions from that house to meet the steamship Beaver, receive, care for and list the survivors of the Leggett and do all things for their comfort, convenience and dispatch; a task Mr. Cherry was busy about from the instant the "Big Three" liner docked.

Everything becomes cloudy and vague from here on out because the newspapers are so focused on the *"wind and seas"*. Within days after the sinking, I read of wind gusts that have magically increased from an estimated one, sixty-knot gust, to a steady ninety-miles-per-hour, and mountainous seas! Less than a week later, a Midwest paper ran an article account where the ship had plowed into massive rocks during the raging storm!

The Japanese warship **Idzumo** which was patrolling off the coast as part of a joint agreement to defend our west coast, since we were at war in Europe, received a distress call from the **Francis H. Leggett**. According to various newspapers around the country this appears to be the only ship that received the final *SOS*, which they said came in around 3:15 pm Friday afternoon. Since they refused to disclose the exact position of the sinking, the newspaper frenzy in the next forty-eight hours accused them of either ramming or shelling the ship. I could not find anything nefarious in their actions and I think I can explain why a final sinking position was never given out.

So, we have a 16-hour window to fill. Sixty-five miles in sixteen hours, averages out to about 4.0 knots, and we need to factor in survivor Alex Farrell's report of strong southerly winds building in the early morning and a fully loaded, but no evidence of an overloaded, ship without a log raft. The articles that were written within thirty-six hours of the sinking and published by the local Astoria papers appear to be the most accurate while later reports become highly dramatized.

I'm an ex-captain and I have a lot of heavy weather sea time from my time spent in the *Bering Sea* so, I can apply my own experiences to the unfolding disaster, and I feel the need to defend Captain Maro who I see being accused of poor seamanship. Obviously, the ship sank, he was the captain, and he went down with her, so he's the easiest scapegoat. Good captains in the coastal trade industry pilot their vessels between destinations that are provided by the office of the owners they work for. They are responsible for keeping the crew inline, proper loading, and safe navigation. If something major breaks, the captain would have notified the home office and made plans to have the ship repaired. All fleets have a fleet manager, it is this person's job to arrange for major repairs. Depending on the size of the company they might also have their own repair facilities and crew or would be able to bargain with existing shipyards in their home port, which in this case would have been San Francisco, for a discount.

Astoria Daily Budget - *Saturday, September 19, 1914*

Reprinted with permission of the Daily Astorian and Clatsop Historical Society which manages historic Daily Astorian news articles.

Steamer Lost and Scores Are Drowned

Steamer Francis Leggett sinks with nearly all on board.

"Accident occurred yesterday afternoon off Yaquina Head—One survivor reaches here with the thrilling story of the terrible catastrophe.

Another victim has been added to the list claimed by the hungry seas and the catastrophe that entailed the loss of approximately 70 lives. The accident occurred about 3:15 Friday afternoon 30 miles northwest by north of Yaquina light or approximately 60 miles south of the Columbia River. When the steam schooner Francis S. Leggett went to the bottom taking with her all but two of her passengers and crew. One of the survivors, Alex Farrell of Sacramento, Cal. a passenger arrived on the steamer Beaver this afternoon and the only other known survivor was onboard the Associated oil tanker Frank H Buck which is outside the Heads and will be in late this evening or tomorrow.

Alex Farrell was badly exhausted as a result of his terrible experience and was taken to Portland on the Beaver, but he was able to tell of the disaster and spoke most complimentary of the work performed by Captain Storro master of the ill-fated craft, and crew in their efforts to save the vessel and her passengers as well as the valuable assistance rendered by Captain Jensen, who with his wife, was a passenger on board. In telling of the wreck Farrell said.

"So far as I know and believe, only one other person besides myself of the 70 or more people on board was saved." He is onboard the tank steamer Buck. Who he is I do not know, but I think he must be the wireless operator, as he was the last person, I saw alive because we had floated close together for hours and until darkness came.

"We sailed from Grays Harbor at 8:30 am on Wednesday morning and there was a full list of passengers, probably 40 and the crew numbered approximately 30 all told. Among the number were six women, a girl, and a boy, including the captain's wife, the mate's wife, and the wife of Captain Jensen. The craft carried a full load of lumber. Almost immediately after leaving port we ran into heavy weather which increased in violence until yesterday morning it was blowing a living gale. The steamer labored incessantly and could make almost no headway. Little alarm was felt, however, as the captain and crew told us that the steamer would weather the gale and there was absolutely no panic even when the final crash came.

Shortly after noon yesterday the crew began to jettison the deck-load and most of the passengers were driven below to keep them out of harm's way.

Suddenly, a terrific sea tore opens a hatch, the water poured in, in torrents and the vessel lurched to one side and capsized. All of this occurred within a few minutes, but in the meantime the crew launched two boats, one containing two women and four men and the other with 4 women and their husbands on board.

It was at that moment that the only excitement occurred. As the second boat was being prepared some men rushed for it, but Captain Jensen made

them stand back, saying he would shoot the first man who stepped aboard until all the women were cared for. The effort was useless, however, for as soon as the small boats struck the water, they capsized and all of them were lost."

Thirty People Sink

"I was standing near the bridge when the steamer went over. I went down with the suction, how far I cannot say, it was a long way and as I came to the surface, I saw the vessels bow stick out of the water and then slowly sink. Fortunately, I was able to grab a floating tie and I clung to it, drifting about, and chilled to the bone by the ice-cold water. Probably 30 people were in sight when I first came to the surface, hanging to pieces of wreckage, but they succumbed one by one until there were only five of us left.

"Of these, one was the wireless operator and the other three besides myself were women. The latter kept afloat until nearly dark when they too disappeared. It must have been about 3:10 in the afternoon when the Leggett turned turtle and it was 1 o'clock this morning before I was picked up by a boat from the steamer Buck and transferred to the Beaver."

I was not injured in any way and indeed most thankful to have escaped alive."

Captain Mason of the steamer Beaver, who brought in one of the two survivors says the first he heard of the disaster was about 3:30 yesterday afternoon. When the Japanese cruiser Idzumo sent a wireless saying that the Leggett had sunk but did

not give the location. About midnight he received a wireless from the steamer Buck saying she was at the scene and had rescued one man. The Beaver hastened at once to give assistance if possible and until 12:30 until six o'clock this morning searched the wreckage for survivors but found none. The only thing in sight were small pieces of lumber and other debris. While the Beaver was there the Buck small boat found the survivor that was turned over to the passenger craft. The Northland and El Segunda were also in the vicinity, but it is not believed that they picked up anyone. A wireless message received this afternoon from the Buck says the man she has on board is too exhausted to talk accepting to say that he is a survivor from the Leggett.

The Francis H. Leggett was a vessel of 1506 gross tons. She was built in Newport News in 1903 and was owned in San Francisco, she was commanded by Captain Charles Storro, one of the best-known skippers on the coast and carried a crew of about 30 men all totaled.

Later—it is now known that the survivor from the steamer Francis H. Leggett who is on the tanker Buck is George Pullman of Winnipeg Canada, he was a passenger on the wrecked steamer."

My Interpretations

The newspaper accounts following the docking of the **Beaver** are when the confusion starts. Many reporters note the much smaller **Beaver** crossed the Columbia River Bar with Alex Farrell onboard on the morning of the nineteenth, but the much larger **Frank H. Buck** chose to wait another day until the storm subsided.

Survivor Alex Farrell is just a young guy and does not have a maritime background, but he had just returned from Central America where he had been working with steam shovels building the Panama Canal, which was officially completed August 15th, 1914. He has been around ships and heavy equipment, so he would have known if the ship was turned around and running with the seas, and it is never once mentioned in any article and the rest of his accounts are much too accurate to miss something this significant. Turning the vessel around to put the seas on the stern is a common and accepted practice in heavy weather if equipment or a load has become unsecured. I've done it myself.

Farrell said that around noon Captain Maro gave the order to jettison the deck load and that included both sides. I'm not sure if he's referring to both sides of the hatch cover, or both sides of the superstructure located amidships, or fore and aft. Ordering a deck load of his employer's money to be thrown overboard is not a decision Maro would make without serious thought and shows the situation is becoming extremely desperate.

During the time the deck load was being removed, Farrell said Jensen ordered all passengers to their staterooms. This tells us Captain Maro was somewhere else besides the pilothouse and he had 1st, 2nd, and 3rd officers onboard that he'd apparently taken with him to the aft part of the ship. This is before the hatch cover is lost. There is something serious happening down below.

Captain Maro could have corrected the starboard list by removing a portion of the deck load but when he ordered both sides cleared, this tells me he wants more freeboard, or the distance between the deck and the ocean, so again another clue that shows the ship is already flooding. This was a desperate gamble that obviously failed because the deck load would have been protecting his hatch covers and Alex Farrell reported it was not much later before a terrific sea tore a hatch cover off and she started to rapidly sink.

In Poelman's account, Captain Maro was seen on the stern, or around the wheel, shortly before the ship capsized and he appeared dazed. I can only imagine what is running through his head right then! In this era, wheel and propeller are interchangeable terminology. Also, there is no mention of Maro being in the water after the ship went down and Poelman said he had seen him holding onto the rail as the ship capsized.

Perhaps, also an explanation why the **_Idzumo_** wouldn't provide an exact position of the sinking, is because the young wireless operator sending out the SOS would not have been trained on how to take a hard fix. Captain Maro had come up from the engine space and at this point with the ship settling deeper into the water there's no way for him to reach the wheelhouse and take a fix, the whole stern area of the ship would be an island at this point.

A fix would be taken in this era by taking a magnetic compass reading of a large known landmark such as a headland. You would then line up your parallel rulers on a paper chart on the compass rose and reverse the reading by drawing a line backwards. One more reading on another known landmark and you get a triangle that gives you a fix. This is also the purpose of the lighthouses, each light house has its own code for the light pattern, and it is marked on a marine chart, the working lighthouses used to be found about thirty miles apart, so you always have a visual fix at night.

Farrell did say the young wireless operator was in the water with him, so he was near his station until the ship capsized. But as I mentioned earlier I doubt he would have been trained to take a fix and simply sent out the obvious message, **_Francis H. Leggett_**-_-We Are Sinking,_" over and over.

Farrell said he was standing near the bridge and I'm assuming on the port catwalk when the ship capsized, and he also said there were about thirty people around him in the water so they too must have all huddled together on the catwalk.

Photo Credits, San Francisco Maritime National Historical Park

This picture of the *Francis H. Leggett* shows the catwalk around the outside and on top of the wheelhouse. In some photos the two small boats or launches shown on either side are missing. Neither survivor Farrell nor Poelman make any mention of these, just the two large lifeboats in the stern so I'm assuming on Sept 18th, 1914, they had been removed.

How and what happened after she capsized provided some big clues and the newspapers left them mostly intact. One of the biggest was how the ship sank. Farrell said he could see the whole keel after she rolled, or turned Turtle, as he described it, the bow then rose, and she slowly sank.

Ships always sink with the flooded ends, or side first, so the last part to go under has the most buoyancy. At this point, I'm sure the hatch cover that was lost was the rear one and the only way for a wave to strike the vessel with enough force to lift the hatch cover off, would be if the ship was laying broadsides to the wind, or dead in the water. Those of us with sea time know when you lose propulsion, boats and ships turn sideways and do something we call wallow. I have not been on a vessel yet that wouldn't do it. The violent movement back and forth is something that can easily snap bindings and chains and destroy a deck load, and I believe this is what he is trying to describe.

(Author's Note: All the early newspaper articles I found in the Astoria library had the captain of the *Francis H. Leggett* surname spelled as Storro and then Moro and I have left them historically intact.

After further investigation I am sure the correct spelling is Maro, and I was able to find him using the search feature on the Ancestry.com website, which I am a paying member of. He was born in Norway May 11th, 1878, and immigrated to the USA in 1895, when he was 14 years old. His name was found on a San Francisco census dated 1900 and his occupation is listed as sailor. In a following census dated 1910 his occupation is noted as mate, and he was living in a seaman's boarding house which was common for the era.

In December of 1912 he wed Ella Frances Baldwin who would have been twenty-two at the time and they settled in Long Beach, California. From then on all census reports list his occupation as Master Seaman. It is notable that directly following the loss of the *Francis H. Leggett* his hometown newspaper listed his surname as Mare. Quoting a wired message from the general manager of the *McCormick* office in Saint Helens, Oregon, which was provided by his grieving young wife.

Mrs. Charles Mare, 15 Linden Ave, Long Beach.

"The only two survivors of the **Francis H. Leggett** *reached Portland today. They tell of the heroism displayed by Captain Mare and his crew. So far as we know at present these were the only two rescued and Captain Mare sank with the ship. Will wire and write later as we get better reports. We share and mourn his loss with you."*

It is easy for me to see why there are so many different spellings of his last name, when even the company he worked for could not get it correct.)

Morning Astorian

Sept 19th, 1914

SHIPPING NEWS

The excerpts below are from the shipping reports, which are in the midsection of the daily morning newspapers.

The steamer Temple E. Dorr arrived in port from Bay City and left up to Portland after a short stay at the Callander dock.

The A. O. tank steamship Frank H. Buck is due to enter port this morning, according to her pilot, Capt. W.H. Patterson, who awaits her here.

The steamer Jim Butler arrived in yesterday from the Golden Gate and went direct to Knappton to begin loading cargo for San Francisco.

Captain Macgenn brought the steamer Breakwater into port on her normal railway schedule yesterday morning at 7:30 o'clock and after a brief business call at the O-W R & N piers, went on to the metropolis.

The steamship Geo W. Eldez with freight and passengers for Marshfield and Eureka came down from Portland at 3 am yesterday and left out within the hour, from the Depot dock.

South-east storm signals were renewed yesterday afternoon and emphasized as to the probability of the gale swinging to the southwest and increasing in severity. All small craft in port are hugging their berths including the Mirene and the Della.

The steamship Beaver, Captain Ed Mason, is due in from San Francisco early this morning and will dock at the O. W. R & N piers, with freight and people for Astoria and Portland.

WRECK NEWS

IS HELD

BACK

Marconi Wireless Company

Suppresses Reports on

Leggett Disaster

MESSAGE TO BEAVER

AGENT IS CULLED

With Country Crying for

Word of Disaster Even

Commercial Use of

Radio Refused

Frank H. Buck, *Naval Command*

Morning Astorian

Sept 21st, 1914

CAPTAIN OF
BUCK TELLS
OF WRECK

Heard Jap Cruiser Notify
Wireless Station
at 2 p.m.

QUARTERMASTER
SAVES POULMAN

Officer Jumps into Sea
With Line and Brings
Survivor on Board in Safety

After Laying off the mouth of the Columbia River for 24 hours on the account of the stress of weather, the Associated Oil Company's steamship Frank H Buck, Captain G.B. McDonald commanding, arrived off this city Sunday morning at 11 o'clock and was promptly boarded by the representatives of the local and Associated Press. E. M. Cherry, Lloyds Agent and the Astoria Representative for the Hicks Hauptman Transportation Company of San Francisco, owners of the lost steamer Francis H Leggett, and others at interest, as it was known the Buck had on board the second of the two lone survivors of that fearful calamity off the lower Oregon coast on Friday last.

Captain McDonald instantly responded to the inquiries of the newspaper men with the following details of his connection with the disaster, his story being quoted literally.

The wireless operator, at 2 p.m. on the 18th, heard a Japanese cruiser notifying the station at north Head of the loss of the steamer Francis H Leggett, below Cape Mears. Immediately on learning of the accident I sent for the chief engineer and instructed him to put on "full Speed" and we rushed to the scene of the disaster, arriving in the neighborhood about 11 O'clock at night. A man was seen with a lifebelt on, clinging to a piece of wreckage, but owing to the high seas running I did not deem it advisable to launch a lifeboat and maneuvered the ship down alongside him. One of my quartermasters by the name of Lars Eskildson, bravely jumped overboard with a lifeline, swam to the exhausted survivor, and tied it to him, when both recued and rescuer were hauled on board and everything possible done for them.

"From papers found in the pocket of the man picked up proved to be George Poelman, of St Cloud, Alberta. In the meantime, with the aid of the ship's search-light another survivor adrift was sighted and I called for volunteers to man the life-boat and the instant response was made by Chief Officer A.A. Sawyer and six seamen, launching the boat, in which process one of the life-savers was washed overboard but was quickly picked up and the second survivor, after a hunt of two hours was found and taken on board the boat and later placed on the steamship Beaver. Too much praise cannot be given the work of these lifesavers. The Beaver had come up in the meantime and it was more convenient to get the man on her than on the Buck, and he was cordially welcomed there, because, even at the early hour in which this work was done, the passengers on the Beaver were all up and crowding her rails, from whence they cheered the work of the rescuers to the very echo.

"One of the survivors having been sufficiently revived to be interviewed, said that when the deck-load of the Leggett was washed overboard the holds immediately filled with water, the vessel going down like a rock, the hatches having never been put on before leaving port; two boats were launched from the unfortunate vessel but were at once capsized there being at one time in plain sight from 25 to 30 people in the water clinging to wreckage in all directions, but dropping off one by one, and in the number I saw two women.

(Author's Note: The above seems a literal joke to any captain in the industry because no experienced captain would leave port with their hatch covers off. This is a joke of stupidity within the industry and to think Captain McDonald would say such a thing is beyond belief and reprehensible!**)**

"The Buck and the steamship Beaver staid in the vicinity until daylight closely examining every cluster of ties and lumber for human derelicts but found no further trace and took up our courses for the Columbia River. "We sighted the Japanese cruiser, Idzoma" at 11 o'clock yesterday morning, off the Tillamook coast, south bound.

"Getting down to actual details I may say about midnight, or shortly before. Third Officer Gibbs of this ship, then on watch, sent word to me in my stateroom that he had heard a cry for "help" out on the sea and I rushed to the bridge to confirm it, and believe me it was a call for help from a pair of powerful human lungs and charged with all the terror one human voice could carry. Ordering the ship to be brought about instantly, I went back to my room and dressed, returning to the bridge to take charge of the rescue as we could make: I knew from the thousands of ties and timbers float about us that we were at the scene of the Leggett's disaster. As the Buck came about, she began to drift down on the voice which became instantly nearer and louder and more appealing, and (illegible) our man Eskildson made what is considered to be one of the finest attempts at rescue work I ever saw, in grabbing a rope and plunging over the side the moment he saw a boat could not be let down: it was a night of heavy storm with a huge sea running and his work will stand high in the annals of life-saving wherever they will be written. When the man was brought on board, we did all in our power to make him comfortable and he is just about the most grateful human being it was ever my good fortune to see and talk to."

George Poelmon the rescued passenger from the Leggett, had the following to say to the reporter from the Morning Astorian, when seen Sunday on board the steamship Frank H. Buck.

"We left Hoquiam Wednesday evening and ran into a storm as soon as we entered upon the open sea. The ship was heavily loaded and made very slow progress through the gale. Sometimes after noon of Friday the deck-load of ties began to slide off and soon the ship took on a heavy list to starboard which gradually became worse. As the passengers and crew had donned life-preservers and most of them were on deck. There did not seem to be much excitement. It was blowing, raining and very cold. I stood in the after part of the ship holding on to the rail. I saw men attempt to launch the lifeboat, but it was so rough that they pulled it back again, and I got out; later the boat was lowered again with several men and women in it. It turned right over the minute it touched the water and I could see the poor people splashing around in the sea. Some got hold of ties and boards, but some just drifted out and disappeared. The engines were running all the time, until the very last. Just before the end came, the whistle gave one short blast and then the engines stopped. Captain Moro was near me then, on the deck, near the wheel: he seemed dazed and stood looking around the deck. I was holding to the rail then when all at once the boat seemed to drop out from under me, but I held on as long as I could and went clear under the water with it before I lost my hold. When I came up, I grabbed hold of two ties and hung on. I looked around me and saw lots of men holding to the ties. One man held up his hand to me and I saw he had one of his fingers cut off and his hand was all bloody. I could hear someone shouting but don't know what they said. It was awfully cold and the people near me drifted away all, but one man and I could see him until it got dark, then I was all alone for a long time. Then I saw the lights of this boat (the Buck) and I shouted as loud as I could. They were not far away, and I shouted again but they went right past me, and I thought it was awful but then they stopped and turned around and came back and one man jumped over-board and tied a rope around me, and they pulled me up on the ship. My pardner was near me when the Leggett went down, and I never saw him again. I came from Whidbey Island where I was working on a farm, and I was going to San Francisco. These people on the Buck were good to me and I'm glad to be alive."

George Poelman is a young Hollander about 24 years of age, medium height, and build; light complexioned and seemingly of quiet disposition. He seemed none for the worse for his thrilling experience except a few slight bruises and scratches received from the floating wreckage during his 7-8 hours in the water. He went on up to Portland on the Buck and his wants will be provided for there by the owners of the lost Leggett.

Photo Credits, San Francisco Maritime National Historical Park

Port stern view of the **Francis H. Leggett** shows the upper handrail where I have George Poelman and Captain Maro pictured, when the vessel capsized. I have Alex Farrell and the young morse code operator, and many others huddled on the catwalk surrounding the wheelhouse. Two groups of survivors, that would be separated by waves breaking through the rear cut outs in the bulwarks, as the stern settled lower and lower into the water.

Again, this picture shows the ship deck loaded and towing a log raft, and as an experienced captain, I don't see the ship being overloaded.

My Take

There's a lot of information here to consider. The *Frank H. Buck* had most definitely received a position from some source. Even though much of the first half of the article is said to be quoted directly from Captain McDonald, I question many parts of it. Since the *Frank H. Buck* and the *Francis H. Leggett* were both homeported in San Francisco, there's a very good chance the captains knew each other. As I have previously mentioned, *Francis H. Leggett* leaving Hoquiam with the hatch covers off is a direct attack against Captain Maro's competency, and I don't think any fellow captain would accuse another captain of this based solely on the account of a freshly revived passenger survivor.

George Poelman's account seemed to be extremely accurate, in my opinion. He mentions how he stood in the aft part of the ship holding to the rail, and that Captain Maro was near him on the deck. This reinforces my theory of two separate groups of survivors, and that Captain Maro had been in the engine room.

We can also rule out engine trouble since Poelman said they were operating until the final moment. Once again there's no mention of Captain Maro trying to turn the ship around, just the deck load sliding off to the starboard side, and finally we have the *Frank H. Buck* laying offshore on account of weather, while it is business as usual for all other ships in the area.

Francis H. Leggett with a full deck load.

Blame Steering Gear

Special to the Ledger

"HOQUIAM Sept 21st---That a break in the steering gear of the steamer Francis H Leggett may have had something to do with her loss with 58 lives last Friday is an opinion expressed here by shipping men. The belief is based on the fact that the steamer's steering gear was in bad shape and had been only partially repaired after breaking down on the way north to Hoquiam on the call before the last one. Chief Engineer Hillman stated at the time the vessel had nearly been lost on account of the steering gear breaking, and at the same time the rudder broke. For a time, the vessel was in a bad way, but temporary tackle was rigged and the vessel was brought into port with it. Partial repairs were made at the time, but the job was not completed, though the officers of the ship were advised they were needed."

*Wreckage from Steamer **"Leggett"** on Nehalem Beach, Mayer*

Courtesy of Oregon Historical Society,

Brubaker Album

People have questioned whether or not Captain Maro would have been able to see Yaquina Head from thirty miles away to take a hard fix. I believe he probably wouldn't have been able to see the lighthouse itself, but it was daylight at the time of the sinking and he definitely would have been able to use his local knowledge to spot Yaquina Head.

This picture shows the head taken about twenty years after the sinking and before the now discontinued quarry had cut a large section of the head away.

Francis H. Leggett Conclusions

All accidents start with a chain of events, or dominoes starting to fall, and in this case, it seems to start with the death of Francis H. Leggett himself. I have always questioned why the fleet manager of *Hammond Lumber* advised to sell the ship even though it was only six years old at the time of Leggett's death. The ship apparently needed some expensive repairs at the time of his death and possibly the Leggett family just sold the ship as is. We will probably never know all the details. At this point I am willing to say towing the incredibly large log rafts damaged the ship in the stern area, hairline cracks in the hull plating come to mind. *Hammond Lumber Company* operated a fleet of ships well into the 1930's, until the completion of Highways 1, or 101, made trucking lumber south feasible. So, the reason for the ship being sold wasn't due to a change in the business model, but likely something specific to the ship itself. Following the sale of the **Francis H. Leggett** there are multiple instances of steering gear failure documented and I am positive this is what happened on the morning of September 18th, 1914. No doubt the early fall gale contributed to the sinking, but the ship should have been able to manage these kinds of conditions as she had done this many times before.

The one-year lease agreement between *McCormick* and *Hicks-Hauptman* would be interesting as to which party was responsible for major repairs. Court filings afterwards show *Hicks-Hauptman* was held liable. It's hard to miss the fact that she sank only eight weeks before the lease was up. My guess is the *McCormick Company* was going to pass on buying the **Francis H. Leggett** or renewing the lease and they were trying to maximize profits with bare minimum repairs for the last eight weeks of the lease. The ship had already cost the owners and insurance company a lot of money following the collision and sinking of the **J.H. Lunsmann** sixteen months earlier, so it is not that hard for me to see them going to extraordinary lengths to reduce their liability. Readers also need to remember this is back in the Shanghai era when things were done differently in the maritime world.

I have also wondered what would have happened if Captain Maro chose not to jettison the railroad ties that were lashed to his deck? They were protecting his hatch covers and would have provided some buoyancy even with a flooded engine room. If he could have kept the ship afloat a few more hours they might have been able to successfully launch the lifeboats. I have been at sea in fall gales in this area and they can be intense but move through quickly, with wind direction starting out from the southeast, and then shifting south, and finally southwest, before dying off.

Cape Meares Lighthouse taken in 1912, or two years before the loss of the **Francis H. Leggett.**

Today the steel stairways have been removed, and also the original entrance, which has been moved to the south side as seen in the photograph. The bracket that once held the stairs and ladder is still intact.

From the collections of the *Tillamook County Pioneer Museum.*

The Final Hours of the *Francis H. Leggett*

*The scenario and final timeline I present below is based on my hundred plus hours of research into the sinking of the **Francis H. Leggett** and my at-sea personal experiences with heavy weather.*

Captain Maro's luck ran out Friday Sept 18th, 1914, in the late morning northwest of Yaquina Head with the patched together rudder. He might have made it a few more miles to the south before she suddenly turned broadside to the gale after the rudder failed and started wallowing heavily, dead in the water. This is when the ***Francis H. Leggett*** unintentionally hove to for the last time and started drifting north at 1.7kts. This would support the original timeline noted in the first article, illustrating the time they passed the *Columbia River* at eight pm the previous night, and had supposedly only made it sixty miles south by adding more speed. In the following articles both survivors recalled the same events and I'm going to stay with this version since these are the earliest known newspaper accounts. Usually, the first report is the most accurate before becoming dramatized.

Around noon on Friday Sept 18th, 1914, Captain Maro realized the situation was much worse than the last time the rudder failed, just two trips prior. He then took the hard fix of 30 nm north by northwest of Yaquina Head and 10.5 miles off the beach and gave it to the young wireless operator, who transmitted the position via Morse Code. He then ordered the deck load to be jettisoned and asked Captain Jensen to look after the passengers and he took most of his crew down into the engine room located in the stern to try and re-rig the broken rudder. At this point some authors have guessed he was swept over, had gone to his stateroom in fear or just froze in the wheelhouse. I totally don't agree with any of this, he needed everyone down below to help save the ship.

He is not seen again until just before the ship sank when survivor George Poelman said he was with him in the area by the wheel. Many authors have assumed this means by the helm, but I do not think so, since the propeller is also referred to as the wheel in maritime slang and most especially in this era when the maritime industry had just made the transition from side and sternwheelers to propeller driven ships.

During this three-hour window the events noted by Alex Farrell and Poelman in articles two and three happened, and around 3:15 pm, the ***Francis H. Leggett*** sank, even though in various publications I've read, some say the final message from the *Idzumo* said she sank at 2:15 pm. Again, all this information is being transmitted by Morse Code, I even noted the symbol for 2 is .. _ _ _ while the Morse Code symbol for 3 is _ _ _ .. a mirror reverses and can be easily mistaken by a young wireless operator under duress. Morse code has to be received, interpreted and retransmitted and it's hardly ever done exactly the same, with each operator making small changes. This kind of wireless confusion was heavily documented following the loss of the *Titanic* just two years prior.

Almost all the discrepancies I see in the newspaper articles are the ones being attributed to Captain McDonald of the *Frank H. Buck* which I have serious questions about when they say he was quoted literally.

Final Resting Place

When I started plotting the possible positions of the wreck according to the historical newspaper accounts, the first thing I noticed was 30 nautical miles (nm) northwest of Yaquina Head and 60 miles south of the Columbia River don't match up, there are miles between these two calculations. The first news article reporting the sinking of the *Francis H. Leggett* gives two positions. One is sixty nm south of the Columbia River while the next paragraph of the same article said 50 miles south.

A Portland account gave the position of the original distress call at 30nm north by northwest of Yaquina Head & 10.5nm off the beach, this changes everything from an estimation to a hard fix, one that could only have come from the *Francis H. Leggett* herself. I plotted fixes and there's a five-mile gap between the two points. I also searched NOAA charts for known shipwrecks in this area, but nothing matched up.

That is when I turned to my Oregon commercial fishing fleet contacts for help finding the wreck. The trawl and shrimp fleets have what are known in the industry as, "hang logs." They tow expensive nets around along the bottom and when one hangs up, they log the position in Latitude and Longitude and these numbers are distributed amongst the fleet. This is the way the industry has operated for decades so each boat will have a list of hundreds of known hangs or obstructions. A patch of hard or rocky bottom will show on the down sounder much darker than mud or sand, and normally when a net travels over a patch of hard bottom you might damage the net and you usually retrieve some rocks to help identify what the obstruction is.

Wrecks are much less forgiving, when a trawl net wraps around a piece of jagged steel it grips the net tightly and is almost impossible to pull up or off with the trawl winches and the nets typically just break off. Fishermen are very leery of getting near these areas and they are well marked on their wheelhouse plotters. If you want to ruin a trip, just lose a net! I spent twenty-five years in the trawl industry and only lost one, and this is thanks to other fishermen sharing their hang logs. When I started in the Joint Ventures following the passage of the Magnuson Stevens Act many of our *hangs* came from Japanese and Korean captains who shared with us.

I gave all my calculations on the last known position of the *Francis H. Leggett*, 30nm NNW of Yaquina Head and 10.5 miles off the beach which converts to approximately N 45 10.23 W 124 13 .50. I then applied the drift rate of 1.69 kts I found in an earlier story to Captain Ethan Bohanan of the *F. V. Arctic Fury*, and he provided me with a well-known, to the fishing fleet, large hang just five miles north at N 45'16. 14 W 124' 15. 79. There have been multiple nets lost on this large, unmarked on NOAA charts obstruction, and I'm about as sure as I can be without a visual identification from a remotely operated vehicle or side-scan sonar this is the final resting place of the *Francis H. Leggett*. It is also almost exactly 60 miles south of the *Columbia River Lightship*!

Again, I have Captain Maro pictured in Morse Code communications with his home office around noon, explaining he lost steering again and he would have given them his position of 30nm NNW of Yaquina Head and 10.5 miles off the beach. That fix could not have come from anywhere other than *Francis H. Leggett* itself in the daylight, and the captain of the *Frank H. Buck* said he went full speed to the given position and saw nothing, but continued north and soon ran into wreckage. Just who provided him with the position is purely speculation on my part.

So, in this scenario, if both positions are correct, which I believe them to be, 30nm north by northwest of Yaquina Head & 10.5 nm off the beach being the first, and 60 miles south of the Columbia River being the second, then it shows both positions to be correct and there is no need to pick between the two. This positions the wreck site about ten nautical miles west of Cape Lookout and about fourteen miles west \ southwest of Cape Meares Lighthouse.

When I ask people "have you ever heard about the *Francis H. Leggett?"* it always draws a blank. I find this incredible, considering its Oregon's worst maritime disaster. Beyond being a history buff, particularly interested in the water and vessels, I believe the people lost, and their families, deserve some kind of recognition. It is my hope that my story helps to get a fixed memorial placed somewhere in this area.

Francis H. Leggett

In Memoriam

The Francis H. Leggett was lost south of Cape Meares
and approximately 10 miles from shore,
this is Oregon's worst maritime disaster.

Captain Charles Maro	Winchman Nils Enges	Fireman G. M. Anderson
First Officer Ole Green	Winchman W. Seller	Fireman P. Burns
Second Officer L. Pederson	Seaman R. Engstrom	Fireman William Sullivan
Third Officer T. J. Ordfeldt	Seaman W. Halvorson	Steward D. Robertson
Chief Engineer A. P. Hielman	Seaman Carl Forsgren	Cook F. Pulsinger
First Assistant J. Reid	Seaman P. Hohns	2nd Cook J. A. Watson
Winchman K. J. Soderman	Seaman G. Lundgreen	Waiter George Hogan
Oiler T. Murphy	Seaman M. Madsen	Waiter Charles Martin
Oiler Thomas Welch	Seaman S. Rallgren	

Note: Was unable to find name of young Wireless Operator

Captain Maro & Captain Mason
of The Beaver

Alex Farrell

Captain Jensen

Passenger List

(Possibly Incomplete)

From Aberdeen

Mrs. Nellie Anderson
Helen Anderson, age 12
Miss Rosie Gomez
Robert R. Hind
Miss Tillie Ingles
J. J. Johnson
J. Jensen
Andrew Paul
George Polk
G. Strake
A. Vandelde
Jules Wunderling

From Hoquiam

Verne Lansing
E. McFalley
J. Ohman
M. Peterson
James Smith
R. T. Taylor

From Seattle

Carl Dale
F. H. Davis
John Engstrom
P. H. Fields
D. A. Goldsmith
John Mares
E. Messner
George Mortimer
B. A. Parks
Mrs. B. A. Parks
H. Poelman
John Reutzner
C. A. Rohrbacker
C. L. Stanley
H. Van Hensen
C. P. Warren
Tom Watkins
Raymond Snedeker
Homer D. Snedeker
Mrs. Homer D. Snedeker

Captain Maro

First Officer Ole Green

This fascinating Oregon story spanning the time from when Andrew Hammond and Simon Benson hatched a brilliant plan to ship large log-filled rafts to *southern California*, to the ***Francis H. Leggett's*** last call in *Astoria* before heading north to *Grays Harbor* to finish off her deck load, and finally to her final resting place about 10nm west of *Cape Lookout,* deserves to be told and honored. Though there have been many great stories about the sinking of the ***Francis H. Leggett***, I hope you have enjoyed my account of Oregon's worst maritime disaster. You don't have to be partial to my version, but we all agree on the final tragic outcome. These people do not deserve to be forgotten, and deserve a lasting memorial.

Trivia

In 1915, the practice of crewing ocean-going vessels with a method known as Shanghai was officially outlawed. This included clubbing, drugging, or providing boarding rooms on credit to men who could then be exchanged to a ship's captain for a cash reward.

On December 30th, 1918. *Hicks-Hauptman Navigation Corporation* was dissolved.

In 1920, the 66th Congress of the United States passed the *Merchant Marine Act*, sponsored by Senator Wesley Jones and is now known simply as the *Jones Act*. This law was created to promote the domestic maritime industry and provided basic protections for the mariners themselves.

After Andrew B. Hammonds' (July 22, 1848-January 15th, 1934) death, his vast timber holdings in the northwest became part of the company we know today as *Georgia Pacific*.

About the Author

My background is in commercial fishing, and I spent over twenty-five years working off the Oregon and Washington coast and in the Gulf of Alaska and the Bering Sea, where I sailed with a 1600tn Oceans Masters license. I learned a lot about heavy weather, and unfortunately, the loss of vessels. The pattern always seemed to be the same, a series of events that led to the sinking, followed by mitigating the loss. It's not good or bad, it's just how the industry works! So, the loss of the **Francis H. Leggett** really hit me, and left me asking myself just how this can be Oregon's Worst Maritime disaster and yet a forgotten story.

I currently live in Astoria Oregon, and during the last five years I have spent a lot of hours researching the incredible history of the Pacific Ocean and lower Columbia River. I enjoy volunteering at the *Columbia River Maritime Museum* where I spend most of my time on the **Lightship Columbia**. Prior to that I spent three years volunteering for the *Astoria Fire Dept.* I'm also a member of *Sons of the American Revolution* where I honor the memory of over thirty of my grandfathers who fought in the American Revolutionary War. To say I enjoy history would be an understatement.

You can contact me with questions at captaindan@samandi.net

For more information you can visit www.samandi.net

From my first book,

Magnuson Stevens: As Seen Through the Eyes of a Young Fisherman

Fall Pollock, Kodiak, Island 1984

I was on the early morning wheel watch when this distress call came in. We were close by, so I got Dave out of bed and then I suited up with my one-use cheap camera in hand. Everyone was off the vessel when we got close, so the emergency was over when we arrived. I do remember hearing the most unbelievable screaming sound as air was being pushed out of the ship and finally quit, when the main hatch cover blew about seventy-five feet in the air!